Dallas
Cowboys
TRIVIA CHALLENGE

SOURCEBOOKS, INC.®
NAPERVILLE, ILLINOIS

Published by Sourcebooks, Inc.
P.O. Box 4410, Naperville, Illinois 60567-4410
(630) 961-3900
Fax: (630) 961-2168
www.sourcebooks.com

Printed and bound in Canada
WC 10 9 8 7 6 5 4 3 2

From the blue star logo to the hole in the roof, from Tom Landry's fedora to all those Lombardi Trophies, the Dallas Cowboys are the standard of excellence in the NFL. They are, of course, "America's Team."

But did you know that when the team was founded, the nickname wasn't "Cowboys"? And do you know who founded them? Or in what year? Maybe that's ancient history to you. Perhaps you started following the Cowboys in the days of Troy Aikman, Emmitt Smith, and Michael Irvin. You even know that as a group they were called "The Triplets." But do you know who came up with that nickname?

Soon, you'll know the answers to those questions and many more. Consider this quiz a fun way to learn the history of the Dallas Cowboys and to know more about all the great players who've worn the star on their helmet.

Do well enough and you might even earn a spot in the Ring of Honor of Cowboys trivia—that is, if you can answer enough questions about the members of the real Ring of Honor. When you finish, come back to this page to see where you rank on this Cowboys scoreboard:

1–50 right: Dave Campo caliber
51–90 right: Chan Gailey caliber
91–125 right: Wade Phillips caliber
126–155 right: Bill Parcells caliber
156–180 right: Jimmy Johnson caliber
181–200 right: Tom Landry caliber

THE EARLY DAYS

1. **The founder and original owner was:**
   a. Tex Schramm
   b. Bum Bright
   c. Jock Ewing
   d. Clint Murchison Jr.

2. **On Dec. 28, 1959, Tex Schramm introduced Tom Landry as the new head coach of the:**
   a. Dallas Cowboys
   b. Dallas Rangers
   c. Dallas Texans
   d. Dallas Titans

3. **What did the team's founder trade for the support of Redskins owner George Preston Marshall in the vote to get Dallas an expansion team?**
   a. $15,000
   b. a first-round draft pick
   c. the rights to "Hail to the Redskins"
   d. three oil wells

4. **The first home stadium was:**
   a. Burnett Field
   b. Cotton Bowl
   c. Memorial Park
   d. Texas Stadium

5. The starting quarterback in the very first regular-season game was:

a. Eddie LeBaron
b. Don Meredith
c. Jerry Rhome
d. Don Heinrich

6. The very first touchdown in club history was:

a. a 75-yard pass from Eddie LeBaron to Jim Doran
b. a 7-yard pass from Don Meredith to Fred Dugan
c. a 5-yard run by Don McIlhenny
d. a 21-yard fumble return by Bob Lilly

7. In their first season, the Cowboys' record was:

a. 0–12
b. 0–11–1
c. 6–6
d. 3–7–2

8. The first win came against:

a. Pittsburgh Steelers
b. New York Giants
c. Philadelphia Eagles
d. Green Bay Packers

9. The Cowboys' first Pro Bowl player came from their first season. Who was it?

a. Jerry Tubbs
b. Don Meredith
c. Bob Lilly
d. Jim Doran

10. In 1960, the Cowboys' franchise application was accepted too late for them to participate in the college draft, so their first pick didn't come until 1961. They spent it on:

a. E. J. Holub
b. Don Meredith
c. Bob Lilly
d Sonny Gibbs

11. **What was Gil Brandt's job before getting into NFL scouting and eventually becoming the first personnel director of the Cowboys?**

    a. computer programmer at IBM
    b. athletic director of Texas A&I
    c. bus driver
    d. baby photographer

12. **When Gil Brandt went on his Kicking Karavan across the United States and into Europe, who did he discover?**

    a. Morten Andersen
    b. Toni Fritsch
    c. Efren Herrera
    d. Dick Bielski

13. **What year did the Cowboys record their first sellout at the Cotton Bowl?**

    a. 1960
    b. 1965
    c. 1970
    d. they never sold out the Cotton Bowl

14. **What year did the Cowboys win their first division title?**

    a. 1964
    b. 1966
    c. 1968
    d. 1970

15. **In 1963, the Cowboys became the sole tenant of the Cotton Bowl when the Dallas Texans became the:**

    a. Kansas City Chiefs
    b. New Orleans Saints
    c. New York Jets
    d. Seattle Seahawks

16. **This player was part of the Cowboys for their first four years. When he retired after the 1963 season, he held the NFL career records for catches and yards. Who is he?**

    a. Bob Hayes
    b. Bill Howton
    c. Don Hutson
    d. Raymond Berry

17. **In 1964, ownership made an unprecedented move by doing what to coach Tom Landry?**

    a. telling him who to hire as offensive coordinator
    b. scripting out the first 10 plays of a game
    c. giving him 10 percent of the club as a bonus
    d. giving him a 10-year contract extension

18. **What player was at the center of an intrastate AFL-NFL drama that involved him signing a contract with the Houston Oilers, only to return the money and eventually join the Cowboys?**

    a. Lance Rentzel
    b. Lance Alworth
    c. Dan Reeves
    d. Ralph Neely

TOM LANDRY AND HIS ERA

19. It's only right that the team's first coach was born and raised in Texas. What was his hometown?

    a. Mission
    b. Tuscola
    c. Austin
    d. Tyler

20. Where did he go to college?

    a. University of Texas
    b. Texas A&M
    c. Baylor
    d. Texas Tech

21. What NFL team did he play for?

    a. Washington Redskins
    b. Philadelphia Eagles
    c. New York Giants
    d. Pittsburgh Steelers

22. Which of these was among his primary positions?

    a. receiver
    b. offensive line
    c. linebacker
    d. defensive back

23. **Landry wasn't sure the whole coaching thing was going to work out for him, so he had an off-season job. Doing what?**

   a. selling real estate
   b. selling insurance
   c. selling jewelry
   d. travel agent

24. **How many seasons did he coach the Cowboys?**

   a. 25
   b. 27
   c. 29
   d. 31

25. **Perhaps the greatest measure of Landry's success was his streak of how many straight winning seasons?**

   a. 14
   b. 16
   c. 18
   d. 20

26. **In that span, how many division titles did the Cowboys win?**

   a. 11
   b. 12
   c. 13
   d. 14

27. **How many times did his teams play in the NFC championship game and its predecessor, the NFL championship game (in other words, the game in which winning sends you to the Super Bowl)?**

   a. 6
   b. 8
   c. 10
   d. 12

28. How many times did they reach the Super Bowl?

    a. 4
    b. 5
    c. 6
    d. 7

29. How many times were they Super Bowl champions?

    a. 2
    b. 3
    c. 4
    d. 5

30. What assistant coach was with him the longest (25 years)?

    a. Ermal Allen
    b. Jim Myers
    c. Dick Nolan
    d. Ernie Stautner

31. How many of Landry's assistant coaches went on to become NFL head coaches?

    a. 4
    b. 5
    c. 6
    d. 7

32. Among Landry's coaching innovations was this defensive scheme:

    a. cover 2
    b. zone blitz
    c. 3–4
    d. 4–3

33. Among Landry's coaching innovations was this offensive scheme:

    a. flex offense
    b. run-and-shoot
    c. multiple offense
    d. double wing

34. Landry also is credited with reviving this offensive wrinkle:

a. shovel pass
b. option
c. halfback pass
d. shotgun

35. Don Meredith retired unexpectedly on July 5, 1969. What other significant event in Cowboys history happened that day?

a. Tom Landry received a lifetime contract.
b. Emmitt Smith was born.
c. Tex Schramm unveiled the blueprint for Texas Stadium.
d. Roger Staubach was discharged from the Navy.

36. How old was Don Meredith when he retired?

a. 25
b. 31
c. 35
d. 41

37. Who were the Cowboys playing when Drew Pearson caught the pass that led to the coining of the term "Hail Mary"?

a. Philadelphia Eagles
b. Washington Redskins
c. Minnesota Vikings
d. New York Giants

38. How many yards did that play cover?

a. 25
b. 50
c. 75
d. 85

39. Who coined the term "Hail Mary"?

a. Drew Pearson
b. Tom Landry
c. Tex Schramm
d. Roger Staubach

40. When Roger Staubach retired after the 1979 season, who took over?

a. Danny White
b. Randy White
c. Steve Pelluer
d. Glenn Carano

41. What team did Tony Dorsett burn on his famous 99-yard touchdown run on January 3, 1983?

a. St. Louis Cardinals
b. Washington Redskins
c. Minnesota Vikings
d. New York Giants

42. What else makes that play so memorable?

a. He also had a 99-yard touchdown catch that game.
b. Dallas had only 10 men on the field.
c. It was the final game of his career.
d. Two Vikings collided trying to tackle him a step outside the end zone.

43. When it was time to announce his starting quarterback in 1984, Landry accidentally named this nonquarterback instead of Danny White or Gary Hogeboom:

a. Phil Pozderac
b. Burton Lawless
c. Tom Rafferty
d. Dextor Clinkscale

44. In 1987, the Cowboys used replacement players during a work stoppage. What "scab" quarterback performed so well for Landry that he played again in 1988?

a. Kevin Sweeney
b. Sweeney Todd
c. Loren Snyder
d. Reggie Collier

45. **In Landry's final season, the Cowboys were 3–13. They actually started off okay, going 2–2. But then 10 straight losses followed. Who was the streak-buster against, and, ultimately, the final team that Landry beat?**

a. New York Giants
b. Washington Redskins
c. Houston Oilers
d. Phoenix Cardinals

46. **When Landry left the Cowboys, where did he rank on the list of most wins by an NFL coach?**

a. first
b. second
c. third
d. fourth

47. **Landry died in February 2000. The following season, the Cowboys honored him by: (Hint: Check out the cover photo of this book.)**

a. wearing black cleats
b. wearing a "TL" sticker on their helmets
c. wearing a fedora patch on their jerseys
d. wearing fedora hats instead of helmets against the Redskins

JIMMY JOHNSON AND HIS ERA

48. **Like Tom Landry, Jimmy Johnson is a Texas native. Where is he from?**
    a. Port Neches-Groves
    b. Port Arthur
    c. Beaumont
    d. Goose Creek

49. **How many times were the Cowboys shut out during Johnson's first season?**
    a. 3
    b. 4
    c. 5
    d. 6

50. **How many times were the Cowboys shut out during the rest of Johnson's tenure?**
    a. 0
    b. 1
    c. 2
    d. 3

51. **How many games did Johnson lose before his first win with the Cowboys?**
    a. 4
    b. 6
    c. 8
    d. 10

52. **Who did his first win come against?**
    a. Philadelphia Eagles
    b. Washington Redskins
    c. San Francisco 49ers
    d. Pittsburgh Steelers

53. Who was Dallas's quarterback in that game?

a. Troy Aikman
b. Steve Walsh
c. Babe Laufenberg
d. Steve Beuerlein

54. In the 1989 Cowboys-Eagles game known as the "Bounty Bowl," Johnson accused Buddy Ryan of having a bounty on quarterback Troy Aikman and _____.

a. Kicker Luis Zendejas
b. Receiver Michael Irvin
c. Running back Paul Palmer
d. Linebacker Ken Norton

55. Who was the starting quarterback in Johnson's first playoff victory?

a. Troy Aikman
b. Steve Walsh
c. Babe Laufenberg
d. Steve Beuerlein

56. Who did Dallas beat in that game?

a. Detroit Lions
b. Chicago Bears
c. Phoenix Cardinals
d. Atlanta Falcons

57. The signature game of Emmitt Smith's career was a regular-season finale against the New York Giants. In addition to his running and catching exploits, what else made it so memorable?

a. Smith's parents were watching in person for the first time.
b. It was the same day his first child was born.
c. He played with a separated shoulder.
d. He played knowing he was having knee surgery the following morning.

THE TRIPLETS

58. **Who coined the term "Triplets" for Troy Aikman, Michael Irvin, and Emmitt Smith?**

    a. Jerry Jones
    b. Jimmy Johnson
    c. Barry Switzer
    d. Nate Newton

59. **How did Troy Aikman depart the Cowboys?**

    a. he was traded to Arizona
    b. he retired
    c. he was released
    d. left as a free agent

60. **Who was the free-agent quarterback signed to replace Aikman but then cut during training camp?**

    a. Tony Banks
    b. Anthony Wright
    c. Ryan Leaf
    d. Quincy Carter

61. **Who led the Cowboys in passing in 2001, the year after Aikman's departure?**

    a. Tony Banks
    b. Anthony Wright
    c. Ryan Leaf
    d. Quincy Carter

62. **Who were the Cowboys playing in the game in which Emmitt Smith passed Walter Payton to become the NFL's career rushing leader?**
   a. Chicago Bears
   b. Houston Texans
   c. Washington Redskins
   d. Seattle Seahawks

63. **How did Smith leave the Cowboys?**
   a. he was traded to Arizona
   b. he retired
   c. he was released
   d. left as a free agent

64. **Who led the Cowboys in rushing in 2003, the first year after Smith departed?**
   a. Richie Anderson
   b. Troy Hambrick
   c. Julius Jones
   d. Sherman Williams

65. **Michael Irvin's career ended because of a spine injury. Where did he play his last game?**
   a. Texas Stadium
   b. Veterans Stadium
   c. RFK Stadium
   d. Giants Stadium

66. **As of 2009, what team has Dallas played against the most in the NFC championship game, counting appearances in its predecessor, the NFL title game?**

a. Green Bay Packers
b. New York Giants
c. San Francisco 49ers
d. Washington Redskins

67. **The Cowboys made the playoffs for the first time after the _____ season.**

a. 1963
b. 1964
c. 1965
d. 1966

68. **Long before they were "America's Team," the Cowboys had a less-flattering nickname. What was it?**

a. "Next Year's Champions"
b. "Chicago Cubs of the NFL"
c. "Dallas Can't-boys"
d. "The Big Teasers"

69. **Among those near-misses were losses in the 1966 and '67 NFL championship games, which would have sent Dallas to the first two Super Bowls. Who did they lose to?**

a. New York Giants
b. Washington Redskins
c. Cleveland Browns
d. Green Bay Packers

70. **The first of those two losses was at the Cotton Bowl. What was the big disappointment for Dallas at the end of that game?**

   a. a quarterback sneak by Bart Starr
   b. a 50-yard touchdown pass from Sonny Jurgensen to Charley Taylor
   c. an interception thrown by Don Meredith
   d. a 72-yard touchdown run by Jim Brown

71. **Just how cold was the thermometer reading at kickoff of the "Ice Bowl"?**

   a. minus 3
   b. minus 13
   c. minus 23
   d. minus 33

72. **Depending on whom you believe, _____ was either shut off by Vince Lombardi or failed because of the frigid conditions during the "Ice Bowl."**

   a. a turf-warming system
   b. heat to the visitors' bench
   c. hot water in the visiting locker room
   d. the exploding scoreboard

73. **When Bart Starr dove in to score the winning touchdown in the "Ice Bowl," which Dallas player slipped on the frozen tundra and missed the tackle?**

   a. Bob Lilly
   b. Jethro Pugh
   c. George Andrie
   d. Chuck Howley

74. What team ousted the Cowboys from the playoffs in 1968 and '69?

a. New York Giants
b. Washington Redskins
c. Cleveland Browns
d. Green Bay Packers

75. The Cowboys finally got to the Super Bowl in 1971, only to lose to the:

a. Baltimore Colts
b. Miami Dolphins
c. Pittsburgh Steelers
d. Denver Broncos

76. Dallas lost that Super Bowl in a painful way. How?

a. interception returned for a touchdown with 11 seconds left
b. missed extra-point kick with 9 seconds left
c. defense allowed a touchdown with 7 seconds left
d. opponent kicked a field goal with 5 seconds left

77. Despite losing that game, a member of the Cowboys was voted the MVP. It remains the only time a player from the losing team received the honor. Who was it?

a. Roger Staubach
b. Chuck Howley
c. Bob Lilly
d. Lee Roy Jordan

78. Only two Dallas players who suited up for that Super Bowl did not get into the game. They were Tony Liscio and:

a. Bob Hayes
b. Roger Staubach
c. Bob Lilly
d. Mike Ditka

79. **The Cowboys finally won it all the following season. What team did they beat in that Super Bowl?**

    a. Baltimore Colts
    b. Miami Dolphins
    c. Pittsburgh Steelers
    d. Denver Broncos

80. **An early tone-setting play in that game was when Bob Lilly chased Bob Griese until he:**

    a. broke his ankle
    b. took a 29-yard loss on a sack
    c. lost a fumble that Lilly return 38 yards for a touchdown
    d. threw an interception that Mel Renfro returned 45 yards for a touchdown

81. **Who was Dallas's starting quarterback in that Super Bowl?**

    a. Roger Staubach
    b. Craig Morton
    c. Don Meredith
    d. Dan Reeves

82. **In the January 1976 Super Bowl loss to the Pittsburgh Steelers, which Dallas cornerback got tangled up with Lynn Swann on an acrobatic catch that became the game's signature play?**

    a. Mel Renfro
    b. Charlie Waters
    c. Cliff Harris
    d. Mark Washington

83. **The Cowboys won their second Super Bowl in January 1978, beating:**

    a. Baltimore Colts
    b. Miami Dolphins
    c. Pittsburgh Steelers
    d. Denver Broncos

84. Which former Cowboys quarterback started that game for the opposing team?

a. Jerry Rhome
b. Craig Morton
c. Eddie LeBaron
d. Dan Reeves

85. Which nonquarterback threw a touchdown pass for Dallas in that Super Bowl?

a. Punter Danny White
b. Fullback Robert Newhouse
c. Running back Tony Dorsett
d. Tight end Billy Joe DuPree

86. Which players shared the MVP award of that Super Bowl?

a. Roger Staubach and Drew Pearson
b. Roger Staubach and Tony Dorsett
c. Harvey Martin and Randy White
d. Cliff Harris and Charlie Waters

87. Six years passed between Landry's first Super Bowl champion and his second one. Only three players were in the starting lineup of both Super Bowls. Which of these was NOT among them?

a. Roger Staubach
b. Cliff Harris
c. Jethro Pugh
d. Harvey Martin

88. In the January 1979 Super Bowl loss to the Pittsburgh Steelers, which future Hall of Famer dropped a sure touchdown pass from Roger Staubach?

a. Lance Alworth
b. Mike Ditka
c. Jackie Smith
d. Drew Pearson

89. **Which Dallas defender knocked San Francisco's Joe Montana to the turf just after he threw the pass that led to "The Catch" in the January 1982 NFC championship game?**

a. Ed "Too Tall" Jones
b. Thomas "Hollywood" Henderson
c. Randy "The Manster" White
d. Harvey Martin

90. **Who was the Dallas defender closest to San Francisco's Dwight Clark when he made "The Catch"?**

a. Everson Walls
b. Dennis Thurman
c. Charlie Waters
d. Deion Sanders

91. **Legend has it that the fate of both franchises turned after "The Catch." So what happened to the Cowboys the following season?**

a. They went 5–11, ending Landry's streak of winning seasons.
b. They went 9–7, preserving Landry's streak of winning seasons but missing the playoffs.
c. They made the playoffs as a wild-card team, but lost in the first round.
d. They returned to the NFC championship game, but lost again.

92. **In the January 1993 Super Bowl victory over the Buffalo Bills, who chased down Leon Lett from behind and stripped him of a sure touchdown?**

a. Pete Metzelaars
b. Thurman Thomas
c. Don Beebe
d. Andre Reed

93. In the January 1994 Super Bowl victory over the Buffalo Bills, Emmitt Smith was named the MVP, but many people consider the real star this defensive player who caused a fumble, returned a fumble for a touchdown, and intercepted a pass:

a. James Washington
b. Darren Woodson
c. Thomas Everett
d. Kevin Smith

94. In the January 1996 Super Bowl victory over the Pittsburgh Steelers, this Dallas player became the first person to win five Super Bowls:

a. Ray Donaldson
b. Charles Haley
c. Deion Sanders
d. Godfrey Myles

95. The Cowboys lost Tony Romo's first career playoff start because of what goof-up?

a. Romo fumbled a shotgun snap.
b. Romo threw an illegal forward pass.
c. Romo botched the hold of a short field goal.
d. Romo called timeout when the Cowboys didn't have any.

THE DRAFT

96. **Of the first seven draft picks the Cowboys ever used, how many were spent on players from Texas colleges?**

   a. 0
   b. 1
   c. 5
   d. 6

97. **In 1964, Tex Schramm may have had the greatest draft ever pulled off. It started with this future Hall of Famer in the second round:**

   a. Lee Roy Jordan
   b. Mel Renfro
   c. Bob Lilly
   d. Rayfield Wright

98. **Also nabbed in that draft was "Bullet" Bob Hayes, the fastest man in the world. How quick was Schramm on the trigger to draft him?**

   a. third round
   b. fifth round
   c. seventh round
   d. ninth round

99. **And, in the 10th round, Schramm snagged:**

   a. Roger Staubach
   b. Jethro Pugh
   c. Don Perkins
   d. Cornell Green

100. Schramm's other famous draft class was in 1975. Why?

a. He got three more Ring of Honor players.
b. Twelve of them made the team.
c. He traded all his picks for Tony Dorsett.
d. He drafted quarterbacks with his first three picks.

101. Schramm drafted several college basketball players who never played college football, like Cornell Green, who became a longtime cornerback, and Pete Gent, who became a flanker before going on to write *North Dallas Forty*. What notable basketball player did Schramm take in the 11th round of the 1967 draft?

a. Wilt Chamberlain
b. Pat Riley
c. Cazzie Russell
d. Lew Alcindor

102. In 1969, Schramm's first-round pick, Calvin Hill, led the team in rushing, falling a few yards shy of the club record, and tied another record with eight rushing touchdowns. So in 1970, Schramm spent his top pick on:

a. Offensive lineman John Fitzgerald
b. Fullback Robert Newhouse
c. Tailback Duane Thomas
d. Tight end Mike Ditka

103. The first time the Cowboys had the No. 1 overall pick, Schramm used it on:

a. Ed "Too Tall" Jones
b. Randy White
c. Tony Dorsett
d. Bob Hayes

104. At the end of the 1984 draft, Schramm spent it on this Los Angeles Olympics star:

a. Mary Lou Retton
b. Carl Lewis
c. Edwin Moses
d. Bart Conner

105. In 1985, Schramm took Georgia Tech running back Robert Lavette in the fourth round. Who did he take in the fifth round?

a. Georgia Tech running back Richard Lavette
b. Georgia quarterback Quincy Carter
c. Georgia Tech offensive lineman Chan Gailey
d. Georgia running back Herschel Walker

106. In 1988, the last year Schramm controlled the draft, the Cowboys' first-round pick was:

a. Ken Norton Jr.
b. Michael Irvin
c. Troy Aikman
d. Daryl Johnston

107. Through the 2008 draft, how many times have the Cowboys used the No. 1 overall pick?

a. 3
b. 4
c. 5
d. 6

108. How many Heisman Trophy winners did the Cowboys draft between 1960 and 2008?

a. 3
b. 4
c. 5
d. 6

109. How many of those did they take in the first round?

    a. 0
    b. 1
    c. 2
    d. 3

110. How many were drafted by Jerry Jones?

    a. 0
    b. 1
    c. 4
    d. 5

111. Who was the only Cowboys' top pick in a draft never to play for the team?

    a. Billy Cannon Sr.
    b. Scott Appleton
    c. Bo Jackson
    d. E. J. Holub

112. In 1984, the NFL held a USFL Supplemental Draft. Who did Dallas take with its top pick?

    a. Nate Newton
    b. Herschel Walker
    c. Doug Flutie
    d. Todd Fowler

COACHSPEAK

113. When Jerry Jones and Jimmy Johnson were teammates at Arkansas, who was on the team's coaching staff?

a. Barry Switzer
b. Tom Landry
c. Bill Parcells
d. Dick Vermeil

114. When Jones and Johnson went through their "divorce," what was Jones' inflammatory line?

a. "Any one of 500 coaches could have won those Super Bowls."
b. "Nobody should have hair that shines more than the Super Bowl trophy."
c. "Everyone knows that I'm the brains of the organization."
d. "Xs and Os are nice, but $s are nicer."

115. Barry Switzer was the first Cowboys coach:

a. not born in Texas
b. who'd never been an NFL assistant coach
c. to coach the Pro Bowl
d. who was an offensive player in college

116. Chan Gailey was the first Cowboys coach:

a. not to win a playoff game
b. with a college degree in astronomy
c. who'd already won a Super Bowl
d. who played minor-league baseball

117. Dave Campo was the first Cowboys coach:

a. who'd coached high school football in Texas
b. never to win a division
c. who's father was an NFL head coach
d. to win a Super Bowl as a head coach after leaving the Cowboys

118. Bill Parcells was the first Cowboys coach:

a. never to win a Super Bowl
b. who played minor-league baseball
c. who'd coached college football in Texas
d. with a college degree in astronomy

119. Wade Phillips was the first Cowboys coach:

a. who'd already won a Super Bowl as a head coach
b. who'd coached high school and college football in Texas
c. named NFL coach of the year his first season
d. who played college basketball

TEXAS STADIUM

120. This player is given credit for saying Texas Stadium has a hole in the roof "so God can watch His team play," but he demurs, saying he was merely the first one who told it to a newspaper reporter:

   a. Burton Lawless
   b. D. D. Lewis
   c. Walt Garrison
   d. Duane Thomas

121. Who headlined the first-ever event at Texas Stadium?

   a. Pope Paul VI
   b. Billy Graham
   c. Frank Sinatra
   d. The Beatles

122. Who was the architect who designed Texas Stadium?

   a. A. Warren Morey
   b. I. M. Pei
   c. F. Lloyd Wright
   d. David M. Schwartz

123. The first touchdown scored by the Cowboys at Texas Stadium was by:

   a. Duane Thomas
   b. Walt Garrison
   c. Calvin Hill
   d. Don Perkins

124. The last touchdown scored by the Cowboys at Texas Stadium was by:

a. Jason Witten
b. Terrell Owens
c. Marion Barber
d. Tony Romo

125. The first team the Cowboys beat at Texas Stadium was the:

a. New York Giants
b. New York Jets
c. New England Patriots
d. Detroit Lions

126. The last team the Cowboys beat at Texas Stadium was the:

a. New York Giants
b. Washington Redskins
c. Detroit Lions
d. Seattle Seahawks

127. Who was the starting quarterback for the winning team in the last playoff game at Texas Stadium?

a. Eli Manning
b. Peyton Manning
c. Matt Hasselbeck
d. Jake Plummer

128. Who was the starting quarterback for the losing team the last time Dallas won a playoff game at Texas Stadium?

a. Randall Cunningham
b. Brad Johnson
c. Jake Delhomme
d. Jake Plummer

129. What season was the Cowboys' final playoff victory at Texas Stadium?

    a. 1995
    b. 1996
    c. 1999
    d. 2004

130. In January of what year was the Pro Bowl held at Texas Stadium?

    a. 1973
    b. 1974
    c. 1983
    d. 1984

131. Other than the Cowboys, what NFL team played the most games at Texas Stadium?

    a. St. Louis/Phoenix/Arizona Cardinals
    b. New York Giants
    c. Washington Redskins
    d. Philadelphia Eagles

132. Two NFL teams never lost at Texas Stadium. This team won the most games there without a loss, going 3–0. Who was it?

    a. Oakland/Los Angeles Raiders
    b. Los Angeles/St. Louis Rams
    c. Houston Oilers/Tennessee Titans
    d. Baltimore/Indianapolis Colts

133. Who was the last performer to sing the national anthem at a Cowboys game at Texas Stadium? (Hint: This is sort of a trick question because instrumentalists performed the two final anthems, so this actually occurred at the third-to-last game.)

    a. The Jonas Brothers
    b. Ted Nugent
    c. Adam Rapa
    d. Demi Lovato

BUCKLE UP YOUR CHIN STRAP

134. Who is "Mr. Cowboy"?

- a. Tom Landry
- b. Bob Lilly
- c. Roger Staubach
- d. Walt Garrison

135. Who came up with the nickname "America's Team"?

- a. an NFL Films producer
- b. Blackie Sherrod
- c. Tex Schramm
- d. Pat Summerall

136. Where did it first appear?

- a. the 1978 team's season-in-review film
- b. the *Dallas Morning News*
- c. during broadcast of Super Bowl XII
- d. during an episode of the TV show *Dallas*

137. From 1960–66, the Cowboys were in the:

- a. Eastern Conference
- b. Western Conference
- c. NFL South
- d. NFL West

138. From 1967–69, the Cowboys were in the _____ division?

- a. Southwest
- b. Dixie
- c. Central
- d. Capitol

139. Since 1970, the Cowboys have been in the _____ division?

a. NFC East
b. NFC West
c. NFC South
d. NFC Central

140. The Cowboys set a record in 2007 by having __ players picked for the Pro Bowl.

a. 9
b. 11
c. 13
d. 15

141. Through the 2008 season, how many Heisman Trophy winners played for the Cowboys?

a. 5
b. 7
c. 9
d. 11

142. The Pro Bowl used to recognize both a "back" and a "lineman" as MVPs. The first Cowboys player to receive either honor was:

a. Back Don Meredith
b. Lineman George Andrie
c. Back Mel Renfro
d. Lineman John Niland

143. Since the switch to a single Pro Bowl MVP in 1973, the first Cowboys player to receive it was:

a. Roger Staubach
b. Tony Dorsett
c. Michael Irvin
d. None

144. **The 1974 Thanksgiving game against the Washington Redskins is remembered for the "triumph of an uncluttered mind," which was when this backup quarterback led the Cowboys to a stunning last-minute comeback victory:**
   a. Roger Staubach
   b. Craig Morton
   c. Duane Carrell
   d. Clint Longley

145. **On Thanksgiving in 1994, this backup quarterback saved the day with the best outing of his Cowboys career:**
   a. Jason Garrett
   b. Wade Wilson
   c. Rodney Peete
   d. Bernie Kosar

146. **This quarterback made his only start for the Cowboys on Thanksgiving 2004:**
   a. Clint Stoerner
   b. Drew Henson
   c. Ryan Leaf
   d. Anthony Wright

147. **Where did the Cowboys hold their very first training camp?**
   a. Dallas
   b. Thousand Oaks, California
   c. Forest Grove, Oregon
   d. Marquette, Michigan

148. **Which of the following has not hosted a Cowboys' training camp?**
   a. Rensselaer Polytechnic Institute in Troy, New York
   b. St. Olaf College in Northfield, Minnesota
   c. Cal Lutheran College in Thousand Oaks, California
   d. St. Edward's University in Austin, Texas

149. **How many different places have the Cowboys held training camp from 1960–2008?**
    a. 4
    b. 6
    c. 8
    d. 10

150. **In the 1986 preseason, the Cowboys played the Chicago Bears in the first "American Bowl." Where was it held?**
    a. Paris
    b. Toronto
    c. London
    d. Mexico City

151. **Who owned the team after the founder and before Jerry Jones?**
    a. Bum Bright
    b. Bedford Wynne
    c. Robert Folsom
    d. Ronald G. Wall

152. **Which team did Jerry Jones look into buying long before he bought the Cowboys?**
    a. Houston Oilers
    b. San Diego Chargers
    c. Kansas City Chiefs
    d. St. Louis Rams

153. **How much did Jerry Jones pay for the Cowboys and the lease to Texas Stadium?**
    a. $100 million
    b. $140 million
    c. $200 million
    d. $240 million

154. **Who declared that Randy White was the "Manster," because he was half-man, half-monster?**

a. Cliff Harris
b. Walt Garrison
c. Thomas "Hollywood" Henderson
d. Charlie Waters

155. **Which player opined that if the Super Bowl is considered the ultimate game, why are they planning on having another one next year?**

a. Don Meredith
b. Thomas "Hollywood" Henderson
c. Walt Garrison
d. Duane Thomas

156. **This player said Super Bowl foe Terry Bradshaw was so stupid he couldn't spell *cat* if you spotted him the *c* and the *t*:**

a. Don Meredith
b. Thomas "Hollywood" Henderson
c. Walt Garrison
d. Duane Thomas

157. **What was Roger Staubach's second career during his playing days?**

a. sold insurance
b. sold real estate
c. bank executive
d. stock broker

158. **What was tight end Pettis Norman's second career during his playing days?**

   a. sold insurance
   b. sold real estate
   c. bank executive
   d. stock broker

159. **Going into the 2009 season, what college produced the most Cowboys?**

   a. Texas A&M
   b. Tennessee
   c. Miami
   d. Michigan

160. **When Ed "Too Tall" Jones took 1979 off, what sport did he take up?**

   a. basketball
   b. boxing
   c. golf
   d. volleyball

161. **Pete Gent wrote *North Dallas Forty*. What former Cowboys player wrote a book called *Any Given Sunday*, and later appeared in the movie by the same name?**

   a. Pat Toomay
   b. D. D. Lewis
   c. John Niland
   d. Craig Morton

162. **Why did Jethro Pugh needed legal intervention to sign with the Cowboys?**

   a. He was underage.
   b. He wasn't a U.S. citizen.
   c. He was under contract with the AFL.
   d. He was under contract with the Canadian Football League.

163. **Which former Cowboys player later appeared on *Survivor*?**
   a. Glenn Carano
   b. Gary Hogeboom
   c. Steve Pelluer
   d. Kevin Sweeney

164. **Which former Cowboys kicker later became a multimillionaire when he and his partners sold Telemundo to NBC?**
   a. Rafael Septien
   b. Mike Clark
   c. Efren Herrera
   d. Danny Villanueva

165. **Who was the super-fan who turned himself into the team's unofficial mascot?**
   a. Rowdy
   b. Crazy Ray
   c. The Big Tuna
   d. Gunsmoke

166. **What year did the Dallas Cowboys Cheerleaders debut?**
   a. 1961
   b. 1968
   c. 1972
   d. 1976

167. **Who led cheers at home games before the Cheerleaders?**
   a. high school boys and girls known as the CowBelles & Beaux
   b. soldiers known as the RoughNecks
   c. enthusiastic fans known as the CowboysCrazies
   d. teenage boys dressed as farmers known as the CowPunchers

168. **What was the first year a Cowboys team visited a president at the White House?**

    a. 1972
    b. 1978
    c. 1993
    d. 1994

STATS AND OTHER NUMBERS

169. Who had the team's first 100-yard rushing game?

    a. Don McIlhenny
    b. L. G. Dupre
    c. Amos Marsh
    d. Don Perkins

170. L.G. Dupre led the team in rushing the first season. How many yards did he have?

    a. 362
    b. 562
    c. 762
    d. 962

171. What year did the Cowboys first have a player rush for 1,000 yards in a season?

    a. 1960
    b. 1964
    c. 1968
    d. 1972

172. Who was it?

    a. Duane Thomas
    b. Walt Garrison
    c. Calvin Hill
    d. Don Perkins

173. **The Cowboys have never officially retired a jersey, but there are some numbers that don't get used often. What is the least-used jersey number?**

    a. 8
    b. 13
    c. 49
    d. 74

174. **Which of the following players did NOT wear No. 88?**

    a. Drew Pearson
    b. Michael Irvin
    c. Antonio Bryant
    d. Mike Ditka

175. **Which of the following players did NOT wear No. 12?**

    a. Kevin Sweeney
    b. Roger Staubach
    c. John Roach
    d. Ron Widby

176. **Going into the 2009 season, what jersey number was used by the highest number of players?**

    a. 23
    b. 62
    c. 79
    d. 81

177. **This player made the NFL's all-decade team for the 1960s, along with Bob Lilly and one-time teammate Herb Adderley, but unlike Lilly and Adderley this guy is not in the Pro Football Hall of Fame:**

    a. Lance Rentzel
    b. Lance Alworth
    c. Dan Reeves
    d. Ralph Neely

178. **How many Cowboys made the NFL's all-decade team for the 1970s?**

    a. 5
    b. 6
    c. 7
    d. 8

179. **Only one Cowboys player made the NFL's all-decade team for the 1980s. Who was it?**

    a. Randy White
    b. Everson Walls
    c. Drew Pearson
    d. Harvey Martin

180. **How many Cowboys made the NFL's all-decade team for the 1990s?**

    a. 5
    b. 6
    c. 7
    d. 8

181. **How many seasons did Emmitt Smith lead the NFL in rushing yards?**

    a. 2
    b. 3
    c. 4
    d. 5

182. **How many seasons did Emmitt Smith lead the NFL in rushing TDs?**

    a. 3
    b. 4
    c. 5
    d. 6

183. **Smith set so many records because of his durability. Over his 13 years with the Cowboys, how many games did he miss due to injuries?**

    a. 2
    b. 4
    c. 6
    d. 8

184. **How many consecutive 1,000-yard rushing seasons did he have?**

    a. 8
    b. 9
    c. 10
    d. 11

185. **Everyone remembers Emmitt Smith passing Walter Payton for the career rushing record. But who did Smith pass for the rushing TDs record?**

    a. Walter Payton
    b. O. J. Simpson
    c. Jim Brown
    d. Marcus Allen

186. **In the 1990s, Troy Aikman not only won the most games of any NFL quarterback that decade, he also set the record for most wins in any decade. How many did he have?**

    a. 85
    b. 90
    c. 95
    d. 100

187. **Troy Aikman never led the NFL in passing yards. What was the closest he came?**

    a. second
    b. fourth
    c. sixth
    d. eighth

188. **Aikman may not have had big stats, but he was certainly one of the most respected quarterbacks of his generation. How many times did he make the Pro Bowl?**

    a. 4
    b. 5
    c. 6
    d. 7

189. **How many times did Michael Irvin lead the league in receiving yards?**

    a. 0
    b. 1
    c. 2
    d. 3

190. **Irvin never led the league in receptions. But how many times did he finish in the top 10?**

    a. 4
    b. 5
    c. 6
    d. 7

191. **In 1999, who replaced Irvin as the top pass-catcher?**

    a. Alvin Harper
    b. James McKnight
    c. David LaFleur
    d. Raghib Ismail

192. **How many times has a Cowboys player been voted the league MVP by the Associated Press, through the 2008 season?**

    a. 0
    b. 1
    c. 5
    d. 6

193. Which of the following had the highest career QB rating?

a. Roger Staubach
b. Troy Aikman
c. Danny White
d. Craig Morton

194. Which of the following had the best QB rating in a rookie season?

a. Quincy Carter
b. Troy Aikman
c. Tony Romo
d. Chad Hutchinson

195. Through the 2008 season, only one rookie ever led the club in receiving. Who was it?

a. Bob Hayes
b. Drew Pearson
c. Michael Irvin
d. Jason Witten

196. Through the 2008 season, who had the club record for most yards passing in a game (460)?

a. Tony Romo
b. Roger Staubach
c. Troy Aikman
d. Don Meredith

197. Through 2008, who had the most career tackles?

a. Bob Lilly
b. Lee Roy Jordan
c. Randy White
d. Darren Woodson

198. Through 2008, who had the most career interceptions?

a. Everson Walls
b. Cornell Green
c. Mel Renfro
d. Charlie Waters

199. **Through 2008, who'd played the most games in Cowboys history?**

    a. Bob Lilly
    b. Ed "Too Tall" Jones
    c. Bill Bates
    d. Greg Ellis

200. **Through 2008, who held the club record for consecutive games played?**

    a. Bob Lilly
    b. Ed "Too Tall" Jones
    c. Bill Bates
    d. Greg Ellis

ANSWERS

1. d	24. c	47. c	70. c
2. b	25. d	48. b	71. b
3. c	26. c	49. a	72. a
4. b	27. d	50. a	73. b
5. a	28. b	51. c	74. c
6. a	29. a	52. b	75. a
7. b	30. b	53. b	76. d
8. a	31. b	54. a	77. b
9. d	32. d	55. d	78. b
10. c	33. c	56. b	79. b
11. d	34. d	57. c	80. b
12. b	35. d	58. c	81. a
13. b	36. b	59. c	82. d
14. b	37. c	60. a	83. d
15. a	38. b	61. d	84. b
16. b	39. d	62. d	85. b
17. d	40. a	63. c	86. c
18. d	41. c	64. b	87. d
19. a	42. b	65. b	88. c
20. a	43. a	66. c	89. a
21. c	44. a	67. c	90. a
22. d	45. b	68. a	91. d
23. b	46. c	69. d	92. c

93. a	120. b	147. c	174. d
94. b	121. b	148. a	175. a
95. c	122. a	149. c	176. d
96. c	123. a	150. c	177. d
97. b	124. a	151. a	178. b
98. c	125. c	152. b	179. a
99. a	126. d	153. b	180. a
100. b	127. a	154. d	181. c
101. b	128. b	155. d	182. a
102. c	129. b	156. b	183. b
103. a	130. a	157. b	184. d
104. b	131. d	158. c	185. d
105. d	132. a	159. b	186. b
106. b	133. d	160. b	187. b
107. a	134. b	161. a	188. c
108. a	135. a	162. a	189. b
109. b	136. a	163. b	190. a
110. a	137. a	164. d	191. d
111. b	138. d	165. b	192. b
112. d	139. a	166. c	193. a
113. a	140. c	167. a	194. d
114. a	141. a	168. c	195. a
115. a	142. b	169. d	196. d
116. a	143. c	170. a	197. d
117. b	144. d	171. d	198. c
118. c	145. a	172. c	199. b
119. b	146. b	173. d	200. a